FRANK M

EGO
ALERTNESS
CONSCIOUSNESS

THE PATH TO YOUR
SPIRITUAL HOME

EGO – ALERTNESS – CONSCIOUSNESS

The Path to Your Spiritual Home

Authored by: Frank M. Wanderer PhD
(info@frankmwanderer.com)
Edited and published by: Ervin K. Kery
(editor@kery.org)
Proofreading by: Melissa Jennewein
(onenomadwoman@gmail.com)

ISBN-13: 978-1523880928
ISBN-10: 1523880929
BISAC: Self-Help / Spiritual

www.consciousnessbooks.cf
www.frankmwanderer.com

EGO = The Unconscious Mind
ALERTNESS = Gate to Infinity
CONSCIOUSNESS = Your Spiritual Home

*

"The truth is that we are the incarnation of Life, we are born into this world as a result of a miracle, and later we are lost amidst the multitude of teachings and dogmas. We identify with our beliefs and we forget who we really are: the pure, unconditioned consciousness. This is the essence of Frank M. Wanderer's teaching" (Ervin K. Kery, publisher)

Frank M. Wanderer Ph.D is a professor of psychology, consciousness researcher and writer, and author of several books on consciousness. With a lifelong interest in the mystery of human existence, Frank helps others to wake up from identification with their own personal history, the illusory world of forms and shapes, and to find their true Self in Consciousness.

CONTENTS

PREFACE

Most people tend to identify with their thoughts and personal histories, that is, with their Minds. A lot of us are not satisfied with what we are, and we would like to have a better and more beautiful personal history. That is why we create a mental image of our desired personal development, and the ways of making the work of our Minds more effective.

In order to achieve the mental image we ourselves have created, we embark on a foolish game, as we attempt to bring our Minds under our own control, and be the masters of our own development. Since we do not know the nature of the Mind, this venture is destined to failure right from the beginning.

This game is foolish, since in fact one half of the Mind attempts to bring the other half under control. Our Mind itself deems our own mental image of our personal development good. At the same time, this half of the Mind deems the other half, the one we wish to change, bad. Mental images fight against each other, trying to overcome each other, using the weapons of selective perception and story fabrication. The struggle goes on, with changing luck, all through our lives. Sometimes we believe that we are making some progress, we are improving, and a few weeks, months or years later we drop into the abyss of despair.

A lot of us play this foolish game all through our lives, because we are unable to recognize the simple fact that *the Mind is unable to overcome itself*. We may, perhaps, with the utmost effort, suppress what we believe is bad in us. That is, however, just a virtual victory, leading us to virtual calm and personal development, because when our power declines, the suppressed forces break out again, destroying all the temporary results that we achieved previously, washing away the results of our personal development.

Nowadays, however, more and more of us begin to realize and experience that we are more than our Minds, more that our thoughts and emotions, and the personal history these thoughts and emotions build up. Our attention is no longer completely engaged by telling our personal history and identifying with that personal history, and we become more and more sensitive to the deeper dimensions of our life. We also begin to notice the breaks between thoughts, and we begin to turn towards these gates leading beyond the Mind.

In these breaks between thoughts, the Mind does not work, it is not there–it simply vanishes. What is left there is the alertly watching Consciousness. If we are able to take roots in that alert Consciousness, we recognize that this watching alertness is tolerant with the Mind and its operations. *We shall see that there is nothing wrong with thoughts, nothing wrong with the operations of the Mind. It is not necessary to struggle against the Mind, as it is not an enemy, only an instrument that, without control, tends to function chaotically.*

This tolerant, alert, watching attitude to the functions of the Mind will give us the ability of stopping our thinking effortlessly. Once thinking has been suspended, the continuous stream of thoughts stop, the Mind itself disappears and stops working.

Now we shall not seek our own identity in an identification with the Mind, since we have found our real center, our real self, our alertly watching Consciousness. We will be aware that thoughts and the Mind have not really disappeared, they are still there, only in a dormant state. Our attitude to thoughts and the Mind will entirely change at that moment. We think when necessary, and when we do not need the Mind, we put it aside. The Mind no longer dominates our life, it is not more than an obedient tool that we use or not use as we please.

That is when we realize how wonderful an instrument the Mind is, and now we are able to use it for its original purpose. And the purpose of the Mind is to serve as a means of connections, to connect us to the world and to each other. Through the Mind, used with alert Consciousness, creative energies are released to the world, and create a wonderful harmony there.

I. THE EGO

The Individual is Becoming Somebody

Our life in this world begins when we are born. It is obvious that we are alive, but we are not yet a personality. At that time only the simplicity and greatness of the present, the existence is known to us.

The society, and its culture, is what shapes us into personalities while we grow up. We become a personality when our Ego is born. This is an inevitable step in the evolution of the Consciousness, so there is nothing wrong with that. The Ego is born, the separate little Self, as a focus of the Consciousness. That little Self obtains experience about itself and the world. In the natural course of evolution and as a result of the experience gathered, the Ego withdraws to give way to the process as a result of which Consciousness awakens to its own existence through a human form.

The progress of this evolutionary process can, however, be impeded by an illusion: the illusion that the individual is becoming somebody, a personality. We begin to become somebody, a personality, when we start to identify with the Ego, with that separate little Self. Under that illusion we believe that the Ego is a reality, and we are identical with the Ego, and the development of the separate little Self is in fact the foundation of our personal development. *Nowadays it is virtually impossible to avoid that kind of illusion, since mankind has lived in it for thousands of years. The deception has become independent, and the illusion of the Ego is now a reality for the entire mankind, including, naturally, us.*

Our identification with the Ego makes us therefore *somebody, a personality*. On the other hand, our identification with the Ego will be the root of all our problems and misery. Since around us everybody considers the Ego as the most important centre of their life, we are also brought up by our parents to have a powerful Ego, a center point in our life, by the time we reach adulthood. It is necessary because our society–and its culture–favors and worships the individuals with a powerful Ego.

Our parents and teachers bring us up in the spirit of the permanent endeavors to become somebody, to become a strong personality, to become somebody different from what we are now (to become bigger, more important and better than other people). That is why we always watch other people and compare and measure ourselves to them. All that time, we also try to adjust our actions and deeds to the expectations and opinions of others. We keep dealing with the past and the future, and we never have sufficient time to stop and notice the immense illusion behind our life.

The Personal History

Everybody has their own personal history. Our parents began to weave our personal history; first they told us who we were, they relayed the rules of living in a community, together with other people within a specific society. Then the little Ego was born in us, and we started to listen to the voice of the Ego that began to tell us our personal history. The inner voice told us a story about who we were and which way our life was heading. We found the story so convincing that it never even occurred to us to question its truth.

Every waking moment of our life fits a personal history with our own Self in its focus. Our life can only be interpreted within the framework of that history. The reason for that is that we identify with the voice of the Ego, the narrator of our own story, so closely that our personal history becomes the foundation of our entire life.

A closer look at that personal history will, however, reveal that our internal story consists of a fabric of experiences and thoughts. Thoughts that explain our experiences, thoughts that we believe and with which we are identified, thoughts that will thus provide the foundations of our self-determination.

Our personal history keeps us under its spell, in a hypnotic state in which all our attention is devoted to the inner voice and the story it tells. In this way we give up our alertness, and the world passes by us because we only concentrate on the elements of reality that appear to confirm our personal history. We therefore lose our grip on the deeper dimensions of life. The deeper dimensions are present in our life, but we lose contact with them because of our lack of alertness.

What is an Ego?

The Ego is the central figure of our personal history, based upon the past and looking into the future. The components of the Ego are thoughts, emotions, memories (with which the person identifies as "*my story*"), fixed unconscious roles and collective identifications (nationality, religion, etc.). Most people completely identify with these components of the Ego, and *for them no self "outside" of this exists.*

The Ego is shaped by the past, determining its structure and contents. The structure of the Ego is an unconscious factor, which forces the individual to reinforce his/her identity by joining with an external object. The content of the Ego will then be the thing with which the individual identifies him/herself (my house, my car, my child, my intelligence, my opinion, etc.). The contents of the Ego (with which the individual identifies) are shaped by the environment and upbringing of the person, that is, the culture in which the person becomes an adult.

The identification of the Ego with things (objects, the person's own body, way of thinking) creates the link of the individual to various things. The Ego (and thus the spiritually unconscious person) experiences his/her existence through the possession of various objects. The satisfaction provided by the sense of possession is, however, short, so the individual usually carries on the pursuit for new objects. There is a powerful motivation behind this activity of the individual, a psychological demand to obtain more, the unconscious sense of "not yet enough," and this feeling surfaces in a want for more. This want is a more powerful driving force for the Ego than the desire to possess. The uneasy feelings, recklessness, boredom, stress and dissatisfaction are all largely the products of the dissatisfied longing for more.

The thoughts such as "it's mine," "I want it," "I need it," "it is not enough," belong to the structure of the Ego. The content of the Ego changes with time; it is replaced with new contents. No content is, however, able to lastingly satisfy the Ego as long as the structure of the Ego remains in its place. The individual keeps looking for something different, something that promises a greater satisfaction, making the sense of self of the individual more complete.

This structure determines the various functions of the Ego. The most important of the functions are the following:

1. The Ego strives to protect, sustain and expand itself,
2. The Ego functions in survival mode.

One of the most important strategies of the Ego to sustain and reinforce itself is the experience of "*I am right.*" This is the identification of an idea, position, or evaluation. Nothing gives the Ego more power than experiencing that "I am right."

One of the favorite self-reinforcing strategies of the Ego is complaining. Complaining implies the sense that "I am right." When another Ego refuses to accept that "I am right," it is an offense to the complaining Ego, which in turn further reinforces its self-awareness.

The statement that the Ego functions in a survival mode means that it continually struggles to remain "psychologically alive," so it regards other Egos as rivals or even enemies. It is the desire of the Ego to be right, and thus overcome the other, ensuring its own superiority.

The Ego is a Small Part of the Personality

If we wish to understand how the Ego works, we must not disregard the fact that Ego is only a small part of our personality. Ego is a part of the personality, and its content comes from our sensory perceptions and memories (our life history and the knowledge and experience gathered throughout our life). *Ego is the thinking, feeling and sensing part.* The part of our Ego we show the external world is termed by Carl G. Jung as *Persona*, the acting personality. That part of the Ego is foregrounded when we are in the company of other people. That is, in fact, the collection of our masks.

A large part of the personality is constituted by the unconscious Ego, termed by Freud as the *instinctive Ego.* That is where our most basic instincts (eating, sexuality etc.) are found, and also the part of the personality described by Carl Gustav Jung as the *Shadow. The" Shadow" is shaped and developed by society, almost simultaneously with our role playing personality.* Children, when they wish to meet their parents'– and through them, society's–expectations, begin to develop these masks. These masks are like what environment shapes them to be. Rejecting certain stimuli offered by the environment triggers the disapproval of our teachers, so the intention to reject stimuli is suppressed. That is how our "shadow-personality" develops. It does exist within our personality, but our education relegates it into our subconscious.

Freud believes that the third important component of our personality is the *Superego*. It comprises the social values that the culture in which we grow up find important. In the course of a long and complicated process these values are incorporated into our personality and manifest as the ideal self (the person we would like to be). These values become integral, inner parts of the personality, and surface as opinion and conviction.

The findings of psychological research suggest that more than 90% of the functions of the personality are unconscious. Large parts of the Instinct-Ego, the Persona and the Superego are unconscious. The functions of the Ego are also largely unconscious.

The Ego is responsible for the integrity of the personality, for our inner well-being. This is no small task for the Ego, as it is constantly bombarded by unconscious expectations from the Instinct Ego and the Shadow, attempting to influence its behavior. It generates anguish in the Ego (that is, in ourselves), manifested as discomfort (we do not feel all right). The Ego wishes to escape from the anguish, so it uses subconscious mechanisms. Such a mechanism is, for instance, projection. The Ego projects the unacceptable desires and features coming from the Shadow and Instinct Ego onto others (e. g. I am not aggressive, you are aggressive). These subconscious, protective and anguish eliminating projections are the foundations of several of the mind games to be discussed later.

The Birth of the Ego

Ego, as the organizing and controlling center of our personality, is responsible for creating a balance between the individual and its environment. In these efforts, Ego is assisted by two other components of our personality: *Persona* (the" role personality") and *the Shadow*. These two components fulfill a protective function, as *the Persona screens potentially harmful effects from the external world, whereas the Shadow does the same with threats arising from the unconscious.* These components together constitute the identity of the person.

A baby does not yet have a personality, an Ego, an identity separate from their mother. For a baby, the world is a mixture of tastes, voices, colors, forms and impressions, the elements of which are indiscernible. *There is no Self and non-Self, a baby still lives in an unconscious unity.* As a consequence of urging bodily needs to be satisfied and unavoidable clashes with the external world, with" reality," the harmony between the baby and the outside world will be disrupted. The baby learns to walk, and the world opens up for them. They learn to speak, which will open up social life. *In this way, the baby will be gradually detached from the mother, and a separate "Self" emerges in them, and the Ego is thus born.*

With the acquisition of the ability of speech, the child increasingly identifies with their name.

"Little Stevie is hungry!"–the child says, and gradually learns the concept of" me" and "mine." The child is increasingly convinced that the more they possess and the more often they assert their own will, the stronger their own personality will be. That is how the Ego emerges, the attention turns away from the Miracle and the Consciousness submerges into that dream. The world is becoming larger and larger for the child, they possess more and more, and the Ego grows and becomes stronger. Then follows the kindergarten age, when the child learns to play and assume roles, thus shaping and developing the Persona, the role personality, creating the beginnings of the masks they are going to wear later.

In the unconscious, the Shadow is being formed in parallel with the masks. The patterns of behavior rejected by the adults in the child's environment will sink into subconscious, as these patterns are in opposition to the role and mask of the" good child." That is how the methods of unconscious operation of the Ego take shape.

The Rise of the Ego

When the child gets to school, they learn more and more–often unconsciously–from the adults, from parents, teachers, and unquestioningly accepts everything told them by the grown-up people that the child considers omniscient.

When the child grows and becomes older, they fully identify with their ideas, name and gender, with the masks they have acquired, their qualifications, titles, job and property, learned stories, and their personal life story will be a part of their Ego, increasing the content of that Ego.

And the Ego wants to possess more and more, wants to become more and more powerful. More knowledge, more faith, more material wealth. The Ego wants to devour more and wants to do it more anxiously. That is how the Ego becomes a tyrant and dominates our life to an increasing extent.

The Ego identifies with the human being, a" special species" that has privileges on Earth where all creatures live, and humans are destined to rule over all other creatures. They want to conquer and subdue nature, then they are alienated and separated from nature, though they should be an organic and inseparable part of it–in fact, identical with it.

Ego (which is nothing but a mental product, a system of beliefs) confronts the deep-rooted, natural program of life, instincts, emotional warning signs, and chases them away, replacing them with neurosis, stress and a burnt-out state. What is more, in certain cases it is even able to destroy the individual in a variety of ways. It also confronts the external world ("Let us conquer Earth!"). The extermination of species, violence, wars and ecological disasters show the path of man on Earth. Terrorists, religious fundamentalists, nations fighting wars of conquests, power maniac politicians and uninhibited business people–they are all representatives of the overgrown Ego. *Our entire culture and civilization rest upon the selfish and possessive Ego and, as the Ego created the institutions of society, these institutions are also the expressions of the Ego.*

The Identification

The Ego develops in the course and process of identification, by our identification with our thoughts, emotions, body etc. *As a result of the identification process we believe that we are this Ego, this mind.* In the previous chapters we saw that the mind, the Ego within it, and the things we identify with, are shaped by the society in which we live. Consequently, entirely different types of Ego have developed in various cultures in various parts of the world.

In most people, the term "Consciousness" identifies with that socially conditioned Ego. For a number of people this identification is so powerful that they are unaware that their life is governed by a socially conditioned mind.

The Mind

A characteristic feature of our Mind is that it keeps roaming, wandering; it operates in something like an automatic mode. Thoughts come and go all the time. If we attempt to suppress them, it is only possible with considerable efforts, and even then for only a short time. In most of our waking time, our Mind wanders either in the past or in the future, in our thoughts we deal with our experience of the past, offenses we suffered in the past, or with our future plans, goals and fears.

Another characteristic of our Mind is that it constantly evaluates things. This means that we do not simply live through our experiences, but we also categorize them as good or bad. We judge everything that happens to us and everybody we meet in our lives. This permanent categorization may easily lead to a distorted perception of the world, as we evaluate our new experiences in these categories. If we find an experience negative, we will tend to keep–and reinforce–that category for similar experiences in the future. Our perception will therefore be selective, and we will only accept the stimuli that reinforces our categorization, and we tend to ignore those that fall outside our usual categories.

The third important characteristic of the Mind is that it permanently produces stories. These stories often have a disastrous end. For instance, I suddenly try to remember whether I locked the door of my home or not. The Mind immediately fabricates a whole story around the idea: I did leave it open, a burglar came, my valuables have been stolen, and the police, instead of chasing the thief, will harass me with their questions. We often experience the endings and emotional consequences of these stories. Other types of stories deals with us, who are we, what we are like, what we should do or should have done. The entirety of these stories comprises our personal histories.

The Conditioned Patterns of Mind

These conditioned mental patterns are realized as various systems of beliefs and patterns of thoughts in our lives. These patterns of thoughts and beliefs are not created by ourselves. They have been handed down to us by our parents, our community and the society in which we grow up, and we have also borrowed some from the media. We very often accept these ready-made mental patterns and beliefs uncritically, without any thinking; what is more, we identify with these patterns that will, in this way, be incorporated into our personalities.

That is how our different convictions have been created over the years, it is how we have created a system of values and beliefs for ourselves, and we now organize our entire life based upon those systems. Those conditioned mental patterns serve as a background to the events that are happening to us day by day. The majority of our worries, desires, pleasures and motivations are derived from those mental patterns and all these, in turn, further reinforce those patterns.

A characteristic feature of these conditioned mind patterns–no matter how different they might be in different cultures–is that *they reproduce themselves*. They therefore produce human replicas that meet the expectations and norms of the society they are born into. They adjust to, and keep the rules of their respective society, and they become effective members of that society. They think, behave and feel as expected from good citizens. In the meanwhile, they preserve the illusion of free choice, since the conditioned mind patterns are, to a certain extent, flexible. Then we identify with the conditioned mind patterns and begin to believe that we know the answer to the question regarding our identity, our goals in life.

The Power of the Intention

If we look around in the world as impartial observers, we shall see that most people live their lives closed inside a hypnotic dream.

From dawn to dusk, from birth to death we rush to achieve our goals, pursuing our desires, and suffer from not having a free moment for ourselves, we are overburdened, and live in constant stress.

What are the reasons for that?

This hypnotic dream is the consequence of the nature of the mind. Once the mind has focused its attention on something, intention automatically appears in us. The intention further narrows down our attention to a specific idea and the desires and emotions connected to it.

From that moment on, our life is not under our control, but under the control of the intention. Apart from the things which are the subject of our intention, everything else is left in the background inside us. Our consciousness is obscured and narrowed down, and the tension of the intention focusing on one specific goal takes control over our actions. With the intention comes hope that some day in the future our intention will come true, we will achieve our goal and we harvest the fruit of our efforts. In the majority of the cases, though, the hope remains futile, because there are so many things we wish to achieve in life, our energies and time are limited, so the majority of our goals will be inaccessible for us. Even if we reach one of our goals, very soon a thousand new ones vie for our attention.

This hypnotic work of our intentions locks us up in the prison of our desires and objectives and makes it impossible for us to return to the Consciousness, to the original state of our existence: openness.

In the Captivity of the Mind

In most cases, our Mind is locked up in the prison of the past by an event, the outcome of which is unpleasant to us. Our thoughts turn toward that event in the past, and we would like to change the course of the events, or we worry what others might think of us because of our improper behavior in that past moment.

Another way of becoming prisoners is when our Mind puts the spell of an imaginary future, or the image of a desired, idyllic state upon us. Then we mobilize all our energies to make those images come true, and we tend to pass by the opportunities offered by the present almost blindly.

Yet another way the Mind chains us to our future is with the constant worry about what is going to happen to us in the future. We are afraid of, or even fear, the future, and our Mind constantly produces scenarios of which the outcome is disastrous for us. We lose our job, we fall ill, our partner leaves us, etc.

A characteristic dimension of the captivity of the Mind is that the Mind is usually rejective, or even hostile, to the present moment. We often think that this or that should not happen that way, I should be somewhere else now, in some much better place. Why do such things only happen to me all the time? Our mind is thus in a constant struggle with the present, and that very struggle is what keeps us in captivity.

Living in the prison of the Mind, we are not in control of our lives, we just drift among the illusions generated by the Mind, and in most cases we are unable to act in the present moment.

The Collection of our Masks

In our daily life we tend to cover our real face with a set of masks. Our personal identity is the collection of our various masks. We immediately put on one of those masks whenever we are not alone. Whenever there is another person in the room with us, one of our masks is automatically fixed on our face, matching the situation and the other person.

We ourselves have created these masks unconsciously, under the influence of our parents and teachers, in the course of our life. As a child we made efforts to meet all the innumerable expectations of society reaching us through our parents and teachers. *Perhaps the first of these masks is that of the" good kid" mask, as we have been conditioned to the behavioral patterns of a good child. Then, as we grow up, the number of our masks begin to increase steadily.*

In our daily life, we need a wide range of masks, as we encounter a large number of different situations and people, and we have a suitable mask for every situation. We tend to behave differently with our boss or with our subordinates, with our children, with our husband and wife, with our friends and with our enemies.

Our identity is therefore made up by the collection of our masks that we show to the outside world, and very often we are not even aware of that.

These mask were imposed upon us by society, and after a while we begin to identify with the masks. Eventually, we have completely identified with the masks.

The Mask of Spiritual Ego

The spiritual Ego is unable to imagine the existence of a wisdom that is not manifested in thoughts, accumulated knowledge and experience. The spiritual Ego attempts to make an image of reality from the accumulated spiritual knowledge and experience, trying to create the mosaic image of Truth. The spiritual Ego, however, always picks the stones for the mosaic from external sources.

During our spiritual journey we accumulate a vast amount of knowledge of the world. From the books read, lectures heard and conversations had, we try to pick the useful and interesting bits of information, ideas, thoughts and theories. The same applies to experience.

We believe that if we gather a sufficient amount of information during our spiritual journey, we achieve something, we improve, we make progress. All the knowledge and experience collected, however, improves the contents of the mind, that is, a part of the spiritual Ego.

When we are interested in spiritual development, we apply the same method. In this way we believe we are richer as we accumulate a lot of information, and that we will have more spiritual experience.

The spiritual Ego attempts to make an image of reality from the accumulated spiritual knowledge and experience, trying to create the mosaic image of Truth.

The spiritual Ego, however, always picks the stones for the mosaic from external sources:

- *Eckhart Tolle claimed the following about it...,*
- *It is very similar to the way Osho argues about it...*
- *As Krishnamurti asserts....*
- *On the other hand, Maharshi believes....*

That is how the mind puts one piece of the mosaic next to the other until it believes that the image is complete, and the spiritual Ego is familiar with the whole Truth. That moment, though, will never come, because the image created from the bits and pieces borrowed from others is not the real "truth;" it is only the truth as the mind imagines it to be. As it is not possible to express the Truth with concepts, the image is false right from the beginning.

Another typical way the spiritual Ego is comparing its own experience with those of others:

- *What was your experience? Oh, that has happened to me, what's more...*
- *I have not seen that; how was it with you?*
- *Just imagine, when....".*

By assembling the mosaic image of our own mosaic of "truth" (our own version of the "truth") from our accumulated knowledge and through comparisons with those of others, we shall not be free and do not get closer to Truth. We have only created a beautiful (or not so beautiful) *spiritual mask.*

Our mosaic image of "truth" is realized as a spiritual scenario in our daily life. There may be a number of selfish motivations behind the hunger for experience and quest for completeness, but the spiritual scenarios are rather standard, so they contain lots of similar elements. Let us see a few of these:

One of the common elements in the spiritual scenarios is that *every spiritual seeker finds himself or herself a philosophy, a study, a Master, who is very close to him/her.* This is the starting point. Some of the spiritual seekers believe that the starting point for them is the teachings of Eckhart Tolle: e. g. the endeavor for finding the Now, the Present. Others are attracted to the teachings of Osho, Mooji, or Krishnamurti, and so on.

The second important common element of spiritual scenarios is based upon this. *The mind creates an image about the philosophy for itself, trying to comprehend it and weave from it the clothes for the spiritual seeker.*

The clothes vary to a great extent, depending on the chosen starting philosophy and Master. But the fabric always consists of the expectations; how I am supposed to behave, what methods I should use in order to see the spiritual experience offered by the philosophy chosen. For instance: how can I be present in the Now in accordance with the teachings of my master?

A common feature of the spiritual garments thus created is that the owners all expect the clothes to elevate them from the ranks of the average crowd, helping them to some imagined beauty, imagined love, imagined happiness, some positive experience, positive identity. The mind in this way covers up the spiritual seeker's desire for unity, replacing that desire with these false emotions. The owner will be attracted to such a nicely manipulated garment, not wishing to take it off and leave it behind, as such an outfit lends a powerful sense of false identity to the spiritual seeker.

The seeker of truth (that is, a real seeker, and not just someone attempting to implement a scenario rich in spiritual experience) will, however see through all spiritual scenarios and the spiritual smokescreen thus created.

The Tricks of the Spiritual Ego

The question could emerge in many of us, whether the spiritual Ego is a supporter or an obstructer of the spiritual development. Can it meddle in the process of spiritual development, and if yes, then how does it do it? The spiritual Ego can interfere with innumerable tricks in the life of the spiritual seeker. These spiritual tricks are manifested in various spiritual mind games. Some of the most important ones are discussed below.

1. Develop your Personality!

The Spiritual Ego says: *"Look for truth! Develop your personality to make it the most sophisticated possible! Be spiritual!"*

The Ego-dominated mind keeps coming up with new and new programs, conditionings: "Do this! Do that! Then all your problems will be solved." *You try to obey, but in the meanwhile you are wasting your entire life.*

Personality development is one of the most dangerous traps on our spiritual journey along the road. The more energy we invest into, for instance, the decoration of our spiritual mask, the more powerfully we will identify with it, and insist on it so desperately that we will be eventually unable to abandon it!

In this way, *self-development only polishes the spiritual Ego shinier and more impressive.* In reality, it is the spiritual Ego that instigates the individual's to start a spiritual Journey on the road. It is a defensive mechanism of the mind! It diverts our attention from the possibility of a real internal change by adding an attractive new mask to our collection!

Be aware that Truth is already there in you, here and now in the present moment! Search will only take truth farther away from you, as it either keeps seeking in the future, or presents old obsolete truths of the past to you.

2. Be Calm and Peaceful!

It is the Ego-dominated mind that longs for peace and tranquility. It wants to be peaceful and powerful so that its inner quiet can open a gate for the Formless. The mind nurtures the unconscious hope that in the Formless it will be able to continue to exist somehow. That is why so many spiritual seekers seek spiritual experiences during their spiritual journey.

In reality, however, inner quiet and spiritual Ego, unity and spiritual Ego are incompatible with each other. Where one is present, the other cannot exist.

The Ego-dominated mind is capable of creating some inner quiet and tranquility, a dead emptiness and, with the effort of willpower, it is possible to sustain it for a while. But it is not the quiet of the pulsating, alive internal silence, peace and tranquility saturated with the joy of Existence. Only a mere image of that kind of peace, created and attempted to be implemented by the mind.

We are only able to recognize the quiet of the union, already present in human beings (as this is their real Self), if we are able to give up the expectations, desires, hopes etc. of our Ego-dominated mind.

3. Get Rid of the Ego!

On our spiritual journey we may ask ourselves the question, *"How can we get rid of the spiritual Ego?"*

Who asks this question? The mind itself, the spiritual Ego. When the mind asks that question, we assume that it cannot be the mind, as the Ego-dominated mind surely does not want its own destruction!

We want to shed the spiritual Ego, so we are deeply involved in various spiritual studies, in search of the method that is applicable in our own current situation and circumstances for weakening the spiritual Ego, which will eventually disappear. *That is how the mind misleads us again.*

For studying spiritual methods and choosing the appropriate one takes time, and time is in short supply. Our real Self does not ask questions, as it does not require answers. It is there, it is present Now. We are only able to find it if we forget about questions and submit to the Self, radiating its light in the Present! *Our real Self is light itself, shining bright!!*

The Sea of Expectations

It must have occurred a number of times in our life that we were supposed to meet so many expectations at a time that we almost drowned in the sea of expectations. At our job our boss wants us to be good employees, good workforce, our colleagues want us to be good colleagues and our subordinates want us to be a good boss. In addition to all this, there are the expectations of the family members, who want us to be a good husband, a good wife, a good child. And we have not yet talked about our own expectations in connection with ourselves. It is not surprising that we find it virtually impossible to meet all the expectations.

Put all the expectations in the light of Consciousness, and examine where they come from and why they have such a powerful compelling force in our life.

The Power of the Situation

All the expectations mentioned above emerge from the immense social space which surrounds us, and is commonly referred to as society. *It is thus fully justified to call our expectations social expectations, irrespective of whether they are in connection with a specific situation or a person.*

The more complex a society is, the more space a specific member of it is supposed to occupy in the complicated system of human relationship. These spaces are called social statuses. Such a status can be of gender (man or woman), family (husband, wife, child, sibling, relative etc.), occupation (teacher, policeman etc.) and of occasion (customer, patient etc.).

Every such occupied status involves a set of rules, the system of expectations that dictate how the individual occupying the status is supposed to behave in a specific situation, how to behave as a man, a father, a doctor etc.

These expectations tell us how we must and how we must not behave in a specific situation and in connection with a specific person.

In the majority of cases, these expectations work unconsciously, almost like automatic programs running in our life. *These deep programs have become a part of our mind in the course of our upbringing, and they are activated by a specific situation in which we are or a person we get into contact with.* Then we put on the appropriate mask, tailored to the specific situation or person.

We occupy several statuses at the same time, so it seems that we drown in the sea of expectations. *It is also common that the various expectations attached to various statuses collide with each other, generating further anxiety and stress for us.*

The Programs of Internal Expectations

As our personality develops, some of the external social expectations become internal ones, and merge into our personality and appear as expectations towards ourselves in our daily life.

Our scruples are derived from these social expectations turned inner ones. Scruples start working when we infringe on a rule acquired from our parents or teachers, and do not behave as we are supposed to. *Everybody knows the unpleasant and compelling feeling that drives us back to the track originally dictated to us by the social expectations turned inner ones.*

Another social expectation that becomes an integral part of our inner value system appears at the level of requirements and demands in our life. *Our parents and teachers wanted us to meet the expectations of a specific status as well as we could. Our desire to meet the expectations is a demand on our side.*

Often we set very high goals and strive to do something perfectly in order to meet our inner demand, to reach that level of requirements. If we perform below our standard requirements, the compelling force appears again, and the unpleasant feeling spurs us to achieve a higher performance, so as to reach at least our standard level.

Since we are unable to be perfect in all areas of life, the unpleasant feelings may become permanent.

The Involuntary Track Dictated by the Expectations

What keeps us on the forced track of expectations, why do not we simply leave it behind?

The dynamizing power of the social expectations is provided by our identification with the internal and external expectations, and we base our identity on them. We identify with our social statuses, with the masks of our roles in our gender, family and occupation. These masks are attached to us so closely that we would not be able to exist without them. We identify ourselves with our internal expectations, and our scruples and level of demands often constitute the cornerstone of our identity.

We are so deeply identified with these social expectations, we do not notice that these very expectations convert us into replicas, fake personalities. *The pages of our personal history are written by these external forces imposed upon us by society, they determine how to see the world, how to think about the world, how to think about it, what to believe in, what is good for us and what we should avoid.*

That is how we have lost our individuality over the years and became unconsciously the victims of a manipulation based upon public agreement. The social expectations have been shaped through a general agreement over the centuries, and became manipulative because we insisted on our identification with a separate state of consciousness.

That is how we jointly sustain this identity, rooted in isolation, this social" creatureness," because, due to our ignorance, we stick to the world of forms and shapes. We are only able to imagine our personal existence in the here and now.

The Mirror of Opinions

"Tell me, what you think about me, what is your opinion about me?" we have asked other people this question a number of times. We were, however, not interested in the opinion of just anyone; we only wanted to know the opinion of others who have been close to us: our family members, teachers and friends. All through our life, we have collected these opinions, we have been staring at the mirror. In the view of what we see in the mirror, we make efforts to find an answer to the most important question of our life: Who am I?

What we have gathered from the opinions received from others, we forged an image of ourselves, who we are and what our mission in life is. We have gradually identified with the image, we believed that the image is really us; we have pinned it up on the wall of our room, and proudly show it to any coming our way: look, that is me.

On the other hand, the image in the mirror has also caused us a lot of worry, since there is always a doubt in us: does that image really meet the expectations of others, do we appear good, decent, religious enough in the eyes of others?

As a consequence, we spend our whole life polishing and improving the image in order to make it look better and better for others. We tend to believe that the best strategy in this process is copying, imitating others. This is a strategy that we use from our babyhood onward, that is how we learn our native language, and that is how we acquire the elements of our culture. Later, when we are older, we continue copying others, since if we follow the ways of those who lead a decent and good life, we cannot be wrong.

Another characteristic feature of our image in the mirror is that it is contradictory by nature. We receive almost as many opinions for as many friends and acquaintances we have. Some may consider us clever, whereas others do not find that the most important feature of ours. It generates a permanent state of uncertainty in connection with the image, that is, in connection with ourselves.

This uncertainty in connection with ourselves shall serve as a basis for our desire to convince other people that the image in the mirror is true, and we really are the way other people see us. If our identification with the image in the mirror -generated from the opinions of others- is strong, it keeps us in a virtually hypnotic state, and we live our whole life under the spell of that image.

It is, however, a gross mistake to believe that we see our real face in the mirror of opinions. No opinion is able to reflect our real self, our real, inner existence, and it is impossible to project our real, inner self onto any mirror.

If we intend to really know ourself, we have to be able to turn away from the mirror of opinions. We should no longer deal with what others think about us; instead, we need to concentrate on who we really are. For example, the real issue for us is not whether others see us as happy, but whether we are really happy.

The mirror of opinions will not release its victim very easily, though. It has been so deeply incorporated into our personality that it is in fact a real part of our personality. Whenever we attempt to turn away from the mirror of opinions, an inner voice, the voice of our consciousness will, speaks to us: what are my parents going to say? What would my wife think about it? This inner voice is very often quite effective, and we are again under the hypnotic spell of the image in the mirror.

The Protective Shield of the Indifferent

The deepest source of indifference in us is the fact that we live as separate and isolated Egos and, most of the time, our attention is engaged by telling our personal history. The fibers of the fabric of our personal history are constituted by our opinions and experiences. We devote almost all the energy of our life to make that fabric more and more individual, beautiful and colorful. We remain indifferent to all the things and persons who do not help us in pursuit of that goal. In the case of most people, the process is unconscious, people do not recognize it, as they tend to powerfully identify with their own personal histories.

In the face of what has been described above, it is clear that once we are able to stop telling our own personal history, and we are able to wake up from the spell, the cloak of indifference may fall from our shoulders. Upon that awakening we immediately find ourselves in Life, in the current of pure, constructive energy. We will be filled with vividness, coupled with creativity, spontaneity and drive. In this way happiness and love are incorporated into our life.

We must therefore wake up from the hypnosis of our identification with our personal life story. Quite a lot of us, however, make the awakening a part of their personal story, and convert the awakening itself into an objective to be achieved in the future. Awakening is, however, not attainable as a part of our own personal history.

Immature vs Mature Ego

What does it mean that the Ego is mature or immature? If you ask yourself the question: *"What do I expect from life?"* and you give an honest answer, the quality of that answer contains the response the question of the Ego's maturity.

The immature Ego is always full of desires, it has ambitions and objectives it intends to achieve, whether these ambitions are of the lowest order (money, power) or of the most sophisticated ones (religious devotion, spiritual self-implementation). Reaching these goals always requires time, so future is always important for the immature Ego.

If the (immature) Ego has spiritual objectives, than it may suspect that all important things take place in the Now, here and now, but the Ego still uses the present moment as a springboard to get to its future objectives. A mature Ego is beyond its desires and ambitions bound to shapes and forms. The realization that achieving the goals and ambitions did not bring it real happiness, made it mature. It may have brought temporary satisfaction, but not lasting happiness.

The mature Ego experienced the nature of desires, the constant variability of the world of shapes and forms, where nothing is lasting, everything is dialectical, changeable. The mature Ego is able to abandon its desires and ambitions, and becomes poor in terms of worldly property.

It is important to know that the immature Ego is only able to imitate that poverty, as it has not yet experienced wealth (whether it is material, intellectual or moral wealth), so there is still a suppressed, unconscious desire in it for those things. Until the desires are satisfied, the Ego will not have a chance to experience the nature of forms, shapes and desires, so it cannot become mature.

The mature Ego, when the question *"What do I expect from life?"* is posed, provides the following answer: *I want to find the real center of my life in order to reach the lasting happiness afforded by the independence of shapes and forms, the joy of existence and the state of unity.* That is the only way an Ego is able to turn towards the center of its own existence!

When an immature Ego turns towards spiritual goals and encounters the requirements of a mind-free state, it starts to play its mind games with which it attempts to bridge the unbridgeable gap between itself and real existence.

An immature Ego wants to live in the shapeless and formless world too, and it wants to be somebody in that world as well! As opposed to it, the mature Ego does not insist on itself, it is pleased to surrender to the process that eventually dissolves it. It gradually abandons identification with the Ego (that is, itself), giving way to the recognition that the Ego is in fact a Consciousness without a form.

The Roots of the Ego

The core of the Ego is the Self, from which "I am" then "I am this or that" and finally "This is mine" emerge. In common thinking, Ego is often identified with its outer cloak only (I am this or that, this is mine). The various mind games come into being because we tend to insist on identifying with that outer cloak. If we give that up, we experience" I am" and will eventually abandon "am" and we meet the "I." That "I" is the reflection of the real Self in the mind. Once we have revealed to roots of the "I," we reach the Self!

After what we have read above, we may conclude that the Ego is not something we have to fight, we have to destroy during our journey, or something we can blame everything on; I would make a faster progress on the spiritual pathway had it not been for the Ego etc. As it was pointed out by Adyashanti, the Ego is not something (a noun) but it is a way of the functioning of the mind (a verb).

This operation of the mind (Ego-ing) labels the ideas arising in the brain and the sensations of the body etc.: "*This is mine*" and "*This is not mine*". This posterior interpretation of the ideas arising in the brain is the Ego! The mind games are the consequences of this method of operation.

It suggests a way of putting an end to these mind games and eliminate this operation of the mind. When we run and then stop, running (the verb) is over. When the brain is quiet (e. g. because it intends to fully experience the present moment) or in a meditation, the mind stops working, and Ego-ing also stops with it. The end product, Ego itself, also disappears!

Jump into the Unknown

But now the time has come for us to abandon all lies, and jump head first into the unknown. Let us imagine for a moment that all thoughts evaporate from our head, and we no longer have any concepts, ideas, etc. there. Our lies are wrapped in thoughts, and they carry the false stamp of truth. The loss of thoughts will scare us so badly because the dream world, giving us a false sense of security, will also disappear with them.

When we are able to break free from the spell of our thoughts, we are surprised to realize that our image that we created about ourself will also disappear with our thoughts. We are then unable to answer the question," Who are we?" If we find an answer somewhere inside us, we are still the captives of our thoughts, the thoughts have not entirely disappeared from our head yet. But once our self-image has evaporated, we may no longer think of ourselves as fathers or mothers, Catholics or Muslims, good or bad.

The disappearance of thoughts leaves a gateway open for us towards experiencing real truth. Together with the thoughts, the Ego, the self also disappears, and the truth of *I am* shines out bright. That is the true fact that we have dressed up into the rags of" I am this or that" over the years. Since our environment has concentrated all their attention on that garment, we wanted to make it more and more sumptuous and beautiful. We were so successful in that work that finally we completely identified with that clothing, and the basic fact of existence sunk into oblivion for us.

In our days, however, the time has finally come to shed our garment of thoughts, and find our real Self in the naked truth of Existence.

II. THE ALERTNESS

.

The Turning Inward

The tiny seed of Truth is found in every human being. Similarly to the seed of a tree, the tiny seed contains great potential. If the spiritual Seeker protects and nourishes that tiny seed, it will grow into the mighty tree of Truth. But it can only protect and nourish it, if it's aware of its existence.

The spiritual Seeker's turning inward is therefore a precondition for the germination of the small seed. Turning inward may be interpreted differently by different people, according to their own conceptual knowledge. In general, turning inward means that the person's attention is diverted from the world of forms and shapes towards their internal world.

In this interpretation, there is a subject who is watching and an internal object (breathing, thought, concept, a conceptual image of God etc.) that is being watched. Here the intensification of the attention is equal to the increase of the duration of the attention. The little seed begins to sprout in the internal silence.

The next level of turning inward is when the attention is not focused on inner objects, but on the Consciousness sensing it. E. g. when somebody is watching his/her own respiration, after a while their attention will be shifted from the act of breathing (which is something outside the subject) to the subject itself (the Consciousness watching the respiration). One is only able to perform it lastingly when their concentration ability is sufficiently strong, trained by watching internal objects.

In this interpretation, intensifying attention means that the spiritual Seeker submerges into this Consciousness to an increasing extent. After a while they realize that the Consciousness they focus their attention on is not yet the absolute Consciousness (at that point a lot of the spiritual Seekers lose their way), but the Ego (the I-concept, body awareness). The little seed is now growing and becoming more powerful.

As the power of attention increases, the spiritual Seeker begins to seek where the Ego is emerging from, and what nourishes that Consciousness. That is how they finally return to the source of the Ego, which is the witnessing Presence, the absolute

Consciousness. *Now the little seed is in full bloom, presenting the spiritual Seeker with its wonderful scent, which is the pleasure of Existence itself.*

When the seed is in bloom, the roles of the personality of the spiritual Seeker, their reactions, the work of the mind continue to exist, but the spiritual Seeker no longer intends to change them. The spiritual Seeker does not want to be performing better or to obtain a better role. They plainly watch their own reactions. They no longer identify with the roles and allow the quality of their reactions to determine their self-image. They learn to laugh at themselves. As Witnesses they see and recognize that the Ego is nothing but a bundle of conditioned patterns of behavior and emotion, and as such, it does not have any particular reality.

The spiritual Seeker realizes that for awakening, the sprouting and blooming of the little seed requires intensity in the Now. What is that intensity provided by? The intensity is provided by the recognition that the spiritual Seeker does not identify with the body-mind complex, but with the conscious Presence of true life. Once this recognition permeates the entire self of the spiritual Seeker, then the intensity necessary for Awakening is ready and provided.

The Downfall of the Ego

The social and ecological crises that threaten mankind and our Earth force us to make a choice. We must reach beyond our Ego-dominated mind programs, because if we fail to do that, we will eventually destroy ourselves and a large part of the world!

The Ego must therefore fall, as it is against the evolutionary development of the Consciousness. The downfall of the Ego may take place in two ways: a beautiful, dignified way or a painful one, full of suffering. But both ways will take us to the same goal: the Miracle, the awakening Consciousness.

We are very well acquainted with the journey full of pain. A basic aspiration of every Ego is *growth*, to become larger, stronger and more solid in the world of forms and shapes. It wants to possess more, to get higher and higher in the hierarchic structure of the world, and it wants to conquer a larger and larger territory. Under the spell of the forms and shapes, the Ego devotes all its energy to make the forms constant, disregarding the only constant law of the forms and shapes: *every form is transient, and everything is subject to birth and death.*

The Ego intends to elevate the forms (including its own form) to eternity, which is impossible. This intention of the Ego will be the source of all sufferings, because its world of forms and shapes shall collapse like a sandcastle after a while, until death snatches away the last of the forms: its body from it. It came empty-handed from Nothing, and that is how it is going to return there. *The only treasure it could take along with it is its wakefulness, but the Ego considers that worthless in the world of forms and shapes, as it is not a means of increasing the tyrannical power the Ego.*

The better, more attractive way begins around the middle of the human life, when the individual, under the effects of their experience, tends to recognize the operating mechanisms of the Ego and realizes how tyrannical the Ego is. *The person then turns away from forms and shapes towards transcendental world, free of forms.* That is what one of the most famous psychologist, Carl Gustav Jung, called the spiritual birth of man.

That spiritual birth starts with the recognition that most people only make *in articulo mortis*: that turning away from the Miracle and identification with the forms and shapes is the reason for all our sufferings. A person making that recognition gradually gives up their identification with forms and shapes, and steps back from the whirling of the world into a more quiet area. In this way they will be more alert to themselves and their environment. The clear sky of Consciousness will be contaminated by fewer and fewer clouds, giving way to the return of the Miracle of Consciousness.

In the space of Consciousness, in the state of pure consciousness the person recognizes and clearly experiences that *Ego is a fraud.* The Ego calls itself real and the only existing" Self," though it is nothing more than a conceptual product, the continually changing content of the space of Consciousness that diverts our attention from experiencing the only reality: the Miracle.

The spiritual" newborn" in the pure state of consciousness, in meditation, in the wakeful state of focusing on itself, seeks and searches that complaining and arrogant, constantly chatting Ego in its mind, but finds it nowhere. The individual penetrates all the way to the source of that voice, but when they attempt to grab it, it slips away and vanishes. *The internal monologue, the voice of Ego stops and disappears, it is lost into No-thingness, and the person experiences that there is no other" Self" but the Consciousness. The individual will then realize that the only natural remedy against the paranoid overgrowing of the Ego is wakefulness and attention.*

This is the beginning of a life of a different quality: experiencing the Miracle, which is salvation for all of mankind. First as prehistoric people we recognized our bodily needs, in the Middle Ages we experienced extreme emotions, in the modern age we worship the power of the mind, and now we are on the threshold of a new period in evolution. We recognize that beyond the realm of sensations, emotions and thoughts there is a wakeful, attentive, loving, conscious, factual" something"–and that "Something," that Miracle is *me.* That is *how the human race, waking to Consciousness from the dream of the Ego, is born again.*

Beyond the Ego

The Ego is not bad, it is simply unconscious. The Ego is the deepest dream of the Consciousness. If an individual is able to notice and observe the functions of the Ego, he or she will be able to transcend it. In that case, the individual who has been looking for a more complete perception of the self will recognize that it has always been there, but the functions of the Ego—identification with objects and thoughts—has pushed it into the background. One of the ways of transcending the Ego is not reacting wholeheartedly to the ever-changing kaleidoscope of thoughts and emotions, but concentrating on the alert consciousness in the background instead.

In most people, the term "consciousness" identifies with that socially conditioned Ego. For a number of people this identification is so powerful that they are unaware that their life is governed by a socially conditioned mind.

Those who are able to go beyond that identification with the mind recognize this state of being socially conditioned, and are also able to leave the social conditioning behind. Such a person will not identify with the mind but, increasingly, with the Consciousness. The Presence shall, therefore, control the mind to an increasing extent and will be manifested through the tranquilized mind.

Wake Up from the Somebody-ness

An illusion may only survive if it is continually fanned and nourished. If we take a look around through innocent eyes (that is, through eyes free of any kind of opinions) we will soon realize how every society nourishes and fans, through its various institutions, the illusion of the separate little Self, the Ego. How they nourish the illusion of" somebody-ness" in us and in everybody else. All that may take place because every society, every culture is based upon individuals, and if those individuals disappear, they wake up from their "somebody-ness," and the former *modus operandi* of that society collapses.

That is why Eckhart Tolle is perfectly right when he asserts that the world can only change from inside. The internal change means that we wake up from our" somebody-ness" and we begin to understand what our mission is in the evolutionary progress of the Consciousness.

We must therefore wake up from the illusion of our" somebody-ness" in order to concentrate our attention on reality. That reality is nothing but the innermost empirical fact in our life, that is, the fact that we live, and we constitute a vibrating Consciousness, full of life. That is the reality that has been shrouded from us by the illusion, the mistake that we concentrated all our efforts on sustaining our" somebody-ness."

If we stop nourishing that illusion, it will vanish after a while. In order to severe the power line of the illusion, we must learn how to notice the vividness and beauty of the present moment. Once we are able to accept the present moment, we are able to accept ourselves and we are able to enjoy the simplicity, tranquility and peace of existence. The Ego and the experience of" somebody-ness" then disappear, and we remain nothing but pure, vibrating energy, Life itself.

Escaping from the Captivity of the Mind

In order to escape from the captivity of the mind, we first need to recognize our fixed mental patterns! If we see and recognize these mind patterns, we can shut those doors one by one, which lead us back to our minds' old functioning.

It does not mean that we need to shut the doors ourselves. The fixed operational methods of the mind cannot be defeated by the works of the mind itself, that is, by effort, practice or our willpower.

When a fixed mental pattern appears, all we need to do is watch how it works, and what expectation activates it. But we do not need to fight it, we do not need to make any effort to neutralize it.

There is only one remedy against them, and that is Sight, nourished by the deeper dimensions of Alertness, and the Sight will bring recognition to us. The power of Sight is that it reduces our identification with our minds, and places us back into our original states of existence, that is, into Alertness.

When we see and recognize how our fixed mental patterns work, the energy supply they receive gradually dries up, since the energy that formerly supplied these patterns now supply the emergence of the deeper dimensions of Alertness in us. In this way, conditioned mental patterns gradually lose their power and they vanish. As a result, the work of the mind that might have appeared chaotic to us before becomes increasingly transparent.

In this way, Consciousness and Presence will increasingly dominate our minds, and they will be manifested in longer and longer periods of silence. That is how the mind regains its original mission, and it will become a means by which Consciousness is able to express itself in the world of forms and shapes.

Eliminating Mind Games

Consciousness is an indispensable condition for us to recognize the spiritual Ego and reach Awakening on our spiritual journey. Otherwise it is not possible to observe ourselves. The witnessing, observing Presence should always be there.

The mind will never understand anything that reaches beyond it. But it tries. In this way, though, it will explain everything from the separate aspect that it currently occupies in the time-space continuity.

When one is able to reach beyond that separate focus point and identification with the mind, that the person will also recognize this conditioned state and will also be able to reach beyond that, too. In that case, the individual will not identify with the mind, but increasingly with the Consciousness. The Presence will gain dominance over the mind to an increasing extent, and will be expressed through the mind.

Beyond the Personal History

The question may arise in us whether we are really identical with our own personal history, or perhaps we are more than that? Everybody has some vague suspicion that our personal history does not reflect reality, and that we are in fact at a deeper level than that.

When everything is apparently all right in our personal history, we achieve our goals, we are happy, and the vague suspicion vanishes entirely in us, and our identification with our personal history becomes more powerful. There are, however, moments in our life when nothing appears to succeed, so we are unhappy and we suffer. The suspicion then reinforces in us, and we tend to believe that we are more than the cluster of thoughts that constitute our personal history. We realize that we are more than mere thoughts.

As long as we insist on our personal history, and on the storyteller, the deeper dimensions of our existence remain unaccessible for us. Not because these deeper dimensions are not present in our life, but because weaving the web of our personal history engages all our attention.

Waking up from the Personal History

If we become aware and conscious of our own personal history that we are telling ourselves, we have a chance to wake up from the hypnotic spell of our personal history.

In order to become aware and conscious of our personal history, we must ask ourself the question," *Who is it, talking in my head, who is this inner voice, telling me my own personal history?"* The only possible honest answer to that question is, that" *I have no idea!"* Any other answer is rooted in the personal history, and as such, it is to be rejected.

The honest answer may easily be a shock for us, completely uprooting our life the way we lived it previously. The more closely we identified with our personal history, the bigger our astonishment may be. We no longer believe in what we have firmly regarded as our own personal history. This experience may, however, lead us to the point of questioning the truth of what we believed to be true in connection with ourselves.

This is the first sign that we begin to wake up from the hypnotic effect of our personal history. Now our attention is no longer fully engaged by our personal history, the storyteller telling us the story, and our identification with the story. We may then become sensitive to the deeper dimensions of our life.

The Magic of the Now

It has happened to all of us that we came under the spell of a moment some time during our life. A beautiful landscape, a sunset, a beautiful piece of art, or the rhythm of music enchanted us. It may even happen that we are just lost in the silence of a peaceful moment.

The common feature of these moments is the mind stops working, the reckless stream of thoughts is suspended. Ego disappears, telling personal history stops, and the line of our accustomed identity is broken. Only the spell of the moment, the mysterious shine of the Miracle remains.

Why is this moment so enchanting, what is its secret?

The secret is that when thoughts disappear, so do our problems and conflicts, and we almost forget about all our sufferings. We virtually step out of the psychological time frame, we stop mulling over injuries of the past, and do not build our identity for the future.

We are awake, only the present moment exists for us. Our soul is permeated by the quiet of the Consciousness and the Joy of the Existence.

Unfortunately, these moments do not last long, because the mind starts working again very soon, and begins to control the moment by categorizing it and giving it a name." *Ah, yes, how beautiful is this sunset"* and the tumbleweed of thinking starts tumbling again:*"It reminds me of last summer, when…"*.

Our alert attention will then turn away from the Miracle, back to the mind, and our ordinary identity is rebuilt in a matter of a few seconds. We return to the psychological time and, embedded into it, we experience our problems and sufferings again. The memory of the moments of the spell is just a transient impression, the unconscious feeling that some miraculous thing happened to us, but we unfortunately missed a chance.

Indeed, we missed the chance of entering through the gate opening in the magic moment and seeing the Miracle behind it, and find our real Self there. It is important to learn how to make use of these magic moments, and when the gate opens up again, we have the courage to ask the question:" *Who I am beyond my personal history?"*

But even then we are only standing on this side of the gate of the Consciousness, we have not yet entered. We can only enter if we are able to answer to any given question,*"This is just a thought, a product of the mind, and has nothing to do with reality."*

If we are able to say no to every answer the mind comes up with, all else we need to do is turn towards the Consciousness in us that is looking at the world through our eyes and is listening to the world through our ears.

Be brave enough to open up for the wakeful, living Spirit living inside us.

Existence without Expectations

When we look at the social expectations in the light of Consciousness, we must ask the question: *are we able to live without expectations, what is a life without expectations like?*

The problem does not lie within the expectations. The expectations are natural parts of our existence in the world of forms and shapes, just as it would be impossible to live as a form without our body. Without expectations we would be unable to exist as a part of the social space in which we live at present.

The compelling force of the expectations are rooted in our identification with the expectations, the fact that we cling to our personal identity and the masks that come with it, and the expectations are a natural part of all this.

The proper question to ask is, *whether we exist at all beyond our personal identity, beyond our masks?*

Our world appears in the space of Consciousness, and the dance of the varied forms takes place in it. Out thoughts, emotions, expectations and everything we sense also appears in that space of Consciousness. That is the space of Consciousness, this Miracle is the only phenomenon which is not a" thing", is a „no-thing", not a manifest object but a space-like, wakeful emptiness in which the image of the world, thoughts and emotions appear.

We, however, in our present, dormant state identify with the appearing content elements of the space of the Consciousness, although our real self is nothing but the very space of Consciousness.

If we give up the efforts aimed at building up our personal identity from the contents appearing in the space of the Consciousness, and instead recognize ourselves as the space of the Consciousness, then–and only then–we are able to exist without expectations.

In an existence without expectations we still continue to meet the basic social expectations rooted in the social status we, for a while, fulfill in the world of forms and shapes. We continue to function as a father, mother, doctor, accountant etc.

At present, the program of our internal expectations have already been dissolved, and we no longer identify with our expectations of the other people.

The Acceptance

As spiritual seekers we sooner or later need to face an expectation–almost a common place now–to accept what is actually happening to us, surrender to the circumstances, since this surrender will be the foundation of our spiritual development. The question may, however, arise in us, whether that surrender and acceptance may really constitute the foundation of our spiritual development?

The acceptance of what is happening to us in a specific moment means that we are able to say yes to the things and circumstances that actually appear in our life. Acceptance, saying yes may, however, have two different backgrounds. One of these backgrounds is that when we internally say no to what is happening to us, but our behavior and reactions suggest that we in fact say yes and accept what is happening to us or around us. There may be several reasons for that: we are compelled to do that, a sense of impotence, or cold calculation, a belief that acceptance and surrender will help us in our spiritual quest. But the pretended acceptance and surrender will only lead to further suffering and unhappiness.

Another reason for the surrender to circumstances is when accepting the circumstances is rooted in our inner freedom. Our inner freedom begins when we recognize the psychological background of saying no. It is because when we say no to some circumstance of our life, we most often feel free and intelligent. We unconsciously believe that saying yes would have been equal to submitting ourselves to that particular circumstance or the intentions of a person. In that case, we would have believed that our liberties were curtailed. The sense of intelligence is afforded by the fact that we often need to explain when we say no, with logical, complex reasons, whereas positive answers are usually accepted by our environment without any further explanation.

In the course of our life, however, most of us have recognized–through experience and at the cost of a lot of suffering–that the freedom of saying no is a mere virtual freedom that is only good for reinforcing our Ego. As separate Egos we often tend to forget the basic fact of life that existence is dialectic. That is, no joy may exist without sorrow, and no happiness may exist without suffering.

This forgetfulness is, naturally, understandable, since we all strive to be happy, to enjoy life, so we bravely say yes to these, but our answer to suffering and unpleasant experiences is generally no. This behavior appears to be perfectly natural and human.

But how would we know that we are happy at a specific moment without ever experiencing sorrow in our life? Would we be aware that we are joyful at this moment, when we have never experienced sadness? Pleasure and grief, happiness and unhappiness are equal parts of the same thing, they constitute the two sides of the same thing; that means that if we fail to experience one side, we will not be able to learn about the other. If we reject unhappiness, we will not have the opportunity to experience happiness.

Only when we are able to recognize this basically dual nature of existence, the fact that happiness is rooted in unhappiness, shall our inner freedom enable us to say yes with pleasure to the things that are happening to us.

Once we have achieved the ability to say yes, our internal resistance to the things that happen to us will also cease, and we become conscious and alert to the present moment, and events emerging from that moment. We shall readily accept anything and everything the moment brings to us, let it be joy or sorrow, because we will be fully aware that all these are parts of the same game. That is the only way of remaining quiet, open and ready to accept things, and in this way we shall be presented with peace of mind and the ability to concentrate our attention.

In that state of tranquility, our concentrated attention will show us what we need to do in the specific moment concerned. Our reaction will therefore be an intelligent deed. Only the readiness to accept things, rooted in inner freedom, and surrendered to the circumstances may become the foundation of our spiritual development.

The Lover of the Silence

The world around us is too noisy, we are constantly surrounded by the murmur of the civilized world. We have almost completely forgotten today, how living a silent life in this noisy world could be. What secret could the silence have?

The mystery of silence becomes interesting for us when we become spiritual seekers. From that time on, we start looking for the essence of life, we wish to find an answer to the question:

" Who am I, and what is my mission on this Earth?"

We first look for the answer in the external world. We try to find an idea, an ideology and we identify with it in order to look for the answers to the questions that preoccupy us and cause that tormenting sense of want that spurred us to embark on a quest for answers.

After a lot of futile efforts we realize that no idea, ideology, teacher or master is able to provide us a satisfactory answer to those questions. We then turn inward, and start looking for the answers in ourselves.

Turning inwards requires quiet and tranquility from us, so silence becomes important for us from that time on. We find a quiet corner for ourselves where we are able to think and meditate without being disturbed. We leave behind civilization, go to the mountains, nature or the loneliness of a monastery.

Here at first we believe that we have found what we were looking for, because the quiet of nature, or the quiet life of a closed community surrounds us, and the silence we have found gives us satisfaction and happiness. If we are able to tranquilize the noisy world inside our head in this peaceful environment, external silence may be followed by meditation after a while. The forced internal silence and temporary tranquility is the result of the suppression of thinking. *This silence is, however, not our own, it is not a part of our soul.*

It is aptly demonstrated by the fact that when we return to the noisy revolving stage of society, we are surrounded by the vivid world of a big city, our hard-acquired tranquility is gone immediately, our cherished silence disappears as if it had never existed. If we are lucky, and the external world remains silent around us, only the silence of our meditation is lost every time when the mind starts working, and thoughts and emotions flood our brain.

All this shows that there is something wrong with us, we were completely mistaken when we believed that the magic power of silence will set us free of ourselves. The problem is that we were looking in the wrong direction when we thought that silence is something outside ourselves, something that we are able to achieve by suppressing the work of the mind.

Silence is one of the qualities of our true Self, the Consciousness. We have therefore never lost it, because we cannot lose what we ourselves are. We need to find our inner Self again by allowing Consciousness to wake up to itself in us.

From that time on the silence will always remain with us, and we no longer need to look for it in the external world or force it upon us by suppressing our stream of thoughts. After that, no matter where we are in the world, even at the noisiest railway station, we will never lose our inner silence, our real Self.

The Spiritual Birth

From the aspect of our spiritual birth and internal development, however, the amount of spiritual knowledge gathered, the spiritual development methods acquired, and the sophisticated spiritual events we have had in our life are all unimportant.

Spiritual birth can only be the result of consciousness. Our internal development therefore does not only depend on our life experience; it depends much more on our ability to divert our attention from the outside world to our internal world. Are we able to turn away from the patterns of Mind, programmed by our Egos, and is there a deep desire to know the true answer to the question" Who am I?"

The patterns of the consumer society are determined to prevent us from making the necessary adjustments in our orientation by gluing our attention to various consumer products or a spiritual development scheme that involves the Ego. A major element of this spiritual development pattern is that we are trying to understand the contents of our Minds, to analyze our thoughts and emotions. Our attention is thus engaged by the various methods that we are using to examine our thoughts and emotions. That is what we regard as our real internal world, and we create the illusion of toiling on our spiritual birth.

From the aspect of our spiritual birth the—often chaotic—world of our Mind and emotions is not our real internal world. Our attention should not be directed to the analysis and comprehension of these; instead, we need to concentrate on becoming conscious of our existence, to find the center of our Self behind our external life and personal history. That is our real internal world.

In the course of our spiritual journey we become conscious of, and alert to that internal center, to that internal world. Once that has been accomplished, our life is placed on entirely new foundations. The Mind stops functioning the way it used to and, together with that, our sense of identifying with the Mind vanishes. The spiritual Ego, our separate little self disappears, and we are permeated by a permanent, light presence. The personality is gone, and what remains is silence and presence, as the real essence of our existence.

From that time on, that will serve as the real foundation for our internal development.

The Gate

The gateway leading us to the deeper dimensions of Life is Alertness, which appears as a result of the release of our attention from the hypnotic state of listening to our personal story. The new Alertness enables us to learn about ourselves without identifying with our thoughts and emotions.

What we first experience in this new, alert state beyond our thoughts and emotions is the completeness of existence. In that state all fragmentation disappears from our life, we recognize the inner spaciousness of our existence, our inner happiness and tranquility. We feel at home in our own skin, and we realize that our alert consciousness is free from all kinds of thoughts and emotions.

We then may decide whether we wish to continue to listen to our personal story, or we move further on, towards the quiet foundations of our existence.

The Alertness

What Does it Mean to be Alert? When the notion of Alertness is mentioned at a conversation, people often tend to confuse it with being awake.

Alertness is, however, not identical with being awake, since being awake is only one dimension of Alertness. It is the outermost dimension of Alertness, its surface only. Three dimensions of Alertness may be identified.

The surface, that is, the outermost dimension of Alertness is when the focus of attention is open the widest. Being Alert means that now, in this very moment, with our eyes closed (or open) you pay attention to the processes of your inner world (bodily sensations, the stream of your thoughts, the shifting of your emotions), and the external world surrounding you (noises, scents etc. from the direct world around you). In such an instant you only focus your attention on what takes place in that very moment.

From the aspect of another, deeper dimension of Alertness comes a quality of your consciousness when you cease to evaluate, qualify and control the experience affecting you at that particular moment (disregard the functions of the mind) and, at the same time, you give up all your desires to control events. You have no expectations in connection with the given moment, you accept what is taking place, without making judgments, what is wrong and what is right for you.

The deepest dimension of Alertness is a state of Consciousness the most important characteristic feature of which is the presence of the observing Consciousness, the capability of Sight. In this state of the Consciousness we, as an external spectator, view what is happening inside and around us, and we do not allow these events to take us with them, to affect us deeper. There is a virtual space between you as the contemplating Consciousness and the experiences affecting you. This space enables you to avoid identification with your experience and to look at that experience as an external spectator. Alertness is, at the same time, Presence, which means that you are not only aware of your current actions, but you are also aware of yourself.

It is only possible to talk about real Alertness when all three dimensions are present at the same time. These are inseparable features of Alertness, that together constitute the state that we hereunder describe as Alertness or Presence.

Awakening from the Stupor of Identifications

On most occasions, one is only able to experience that state of Consciousness free of identifications for very brief periods only. This is, however, one of the most wonderful and certainly one of the most important experiences in our life. It wakes us up, in fact shakes us out of the stupor of identifications.

Once we have had that experience, our alertness will increase, and we will pay more and more attention to the present moment. When we are alert and shift the center of our existence into the" here and now," our identification with the forms and shapes will further loosen. Such moments may therefore appear more and more frequently in our life. As we are bound to the forms and shapes to a lesser and lesser degree, the periods and intensity of these experiences increases. In the end it will remain the only reality for us.

Self-Examination vs. Self-Research

One of the most important things in your life should be knowing yourself. Your first and foremost task would be to find an answer to the most elementary question in life: *Who am I?*

In order to be able to answer that question, first you need to find the person who has suffered the experience of the world of forms and shapes, you need to find the experiencer! To that end, you need to do self-research.

It is very important, however, that self-research is not to be confused with self-examination. *Self-examination* always deals with the contents of the mind, it intends to classify and understand those contents. In other words: the mind is examining itself.

Self-research is, on the other hand, is a way out of your personal history and thus from your mind, in order to show you who you really are. It will take you back to your real Self.

At present you have an image of yourself, deeply imprinted by your upbringing, and you believe that you know who you are. This is entirely natural for you, an unquestionable experience.

You are the actual person who experiences the suffering generated by the mental patterns, you believe that you are the one who suffers, that is your experience. During meditation, during your stay in the state of "I am," you also experience that as a Consciousness, you are also independent of the works of mind.

That is how you oscillate between Alertness and sleeping, between something and nothing. If Alertness declines and you fall into a nap, you are again somebody. When Alertness has the upper hand, you are again the free space of Consciousness.

Most people who are in the process of waking up undergo that oscillation; we may therefore claim that it is a part of awakening up. Self-research is the best way of overcoming the alternation of the states of consciousness.

Self-Research

In the course of self-research you question your basic assumption that you are something or somebody. You are doing that by attempting to find the one you have thought yourself to have been.

You are only able to successfully accomplish that if the deeper dimensions of Alertness appear in you, and you have experience with these dimensions. If your Alertness is not at the desired level, self-research may easily and unnoticed slip into self-examination that will certainly take you back into a nice spiritual dream.

How is the self-research to be carried out?

Self-research is a permanent readiness to find the person behind every experience that you suffer. Find out, who the person is who actually experiences that occurrence? Who are those who have expectations in connection with the specific situation or person?

You do not need to ask too many questions, and the questions themselves will have a power. When you seek all that, during your quest, vast energies are released, and that energy enables the deeper dimensions of Alertness to become stronger in you.

Under the effect of the increasing Alertness you will recognize that there is nothing there, nothing tangible and experience-able, only the works of the mind and the thoughts feeding it. The experiencer is but a thought without individual life and identity. It receives all its strength from you, from your Consciousness, because you identified with it and believed in it.

The End of Self-Research

Self-research ends in that effortless Alertness, and nothing is left of what you formerly regarded as yourself. Only the empty space is left, with no limits and borders around it, there are no intentions and desires. That space does not stick to, or identify with anything.

If you examine that apparently empty space, you will discover that it is not entirely empty. It is full of consciousness, which is radiating pure peace and natural joy.

At that moment you realize that you have arrived home. Whatever takes place in the space within you, you only need to experience it. You need to experience everything that life provides then and there, because the next moment is entirely new, and does not have any relevance to the previous one.

The Intensity of Being

In that state of Consciousness you are free of any thoughts and the identification with those thoughts. There are no judgments or categorization; you no longer struggle with emotions and thoughts. All the three dimensions of Alertness are there, full-fledged, in you, and you are Alertness itself.

Alertness is the intensity of Existence, its highest possible intensity.

Now you experience yourself as the space of Alertness, Consciousness, and by the grace of the power of Sight you are able to see what is happening in that space. You, as an eyewitness, contemplate the work of your mind as thoughts and emotions manifest in it, stay there for a while, and then vanish. They do the dance of the forms and shapes in the space of Consciousness that in fact you are yourself.

You no longer meditate, you merely Exist. You do not stay in life, but in Existence. Staying in the Existence is recognized by seeing that the world is a Oneness. You do not identify yourself as an individual separated from the other creatures, but you see all the creatures of the world in yourself, and you discover yourself in every other creature in the world.

You recognize that identification with the immortal creature that you are with the body and mind is not a part of a devilish plot. It is, instead, a station in the evolution of the Consciousness. The purpose is that you should recognize yourself through your own experience; you should wake up from the dream of forms and shapes. That is how a human being is able to return to their real self.

Now you know that you are free, and nothing has ever been created but You, and only the Consciousness awakened to its own existence exists.

III. THE CONSCIOUSNESS

The Nature of Consciousness

When we are asked what we find the most important thing in our life, the most of us would be able to answer the question. We would, naturally, come up with different answers, but that is not the point; the point is that we are able to answer. But as long as we are able to answer, we remain detached from the higher levels of Consciousness. How is that possible?

If we wish to find out how that is possible, we must first examine the nature of higher Consciousness. A number of people have experienced those higher levels, and there are thousands of reports about that state of Consciousness.

Still, if we penetrate deep into that experience, we find that no higher levels of Consciousness exist, only Consciousness itself. That Consciousness has only two states that we are able to experience: one identified with various forms and shapes, and one that is free of forms and shapes.

The Consciousness Identified with Forms and Shapes

What does this identification mean? It means that we identify with a form (e. g. our name) that originally did not belong to us (we are all born without a name), but through identification this specific form has become a part of our existence.

When the Consciousness identifies with a form, the Ego appears. The Ego always means some sort of an identification, self-determination (I am a man, I am a father, I am an English person, I am Christian etc.) The Ego therefore rests upon our identification with things that are important for our ego. If I am able to answer the question," What is important for me?" I am in the state of identification with the forms and shapes.

This state of Consciousness is always restrictive and exclusive. Identification is always preceded by a process of selection: this thing–this form–is important for me, whereas that one is not. We usually choose the forms and shapes that we find beautiful, good and valuable, since these are expected to make us beautiful, good and valuable people. Selection always comes hand in hand with anxiety and fear that we may loose what is important for us and, together with those things, we may loose ourselves.

The process of identification does not stop just because we have become spiritual helpers. But now different things are becoming important for us, for instance the extended state of Consciousness or the experience of the astral projection. At that state of Consciousness, we identify with these experiences, these are the factors that are important for us, they provide the identity of our spiritual Ego. Nothing has really changed, apart from the forms and shapes we identify with.

The Consciousness Free from Forms and Shapes

There are moments in everybody's life when our identification with the forms and shapes loosens a little bit for a short while, and in that instant we may experience an entirely different state of Consciousness.

When our identification with a form ceases, a new space is generated between us and the form and we are able to see and recognize that we are not identical with that form. With the dissolution of the identification, the Ego also disappears. When we are in that state of Consciousness and we are asked what we find important in life, we are simply unable to answer the question, as everything that we formerly regarded as important vanished together with the Ego. Still, we sense that we are alive, and we did not disappear with the Ego.

What we then experience may perhaps be best termed as Being. There is only the pure existence, we are eyewitnesses, contemplating the dance of forms and shapes around us. We do not identify with anything, we are a Consciousness free of the obligation to make choices. We are free and independent of forms and shapes and of the necessity of choosing from them. All our suffering and problems have vanished, we are surrounded by peace and tranquility.

The Evolution of Consciousness

There are three transformational processes within the evolution of the Consciousness. These are, in fact, three levels of development. At these different levels of development the state and functions of the Consciousness show entirely different signs. If we are aware of these characteristic signs, we may easily recognize what state of development of the Consciousness we are in: ordinary Consciousness, awakening or the level of complete freedom.

The Level of Ordinary Consciousness

This is the lowest level of the evolutionary process of the Consciousness. Ordinary Consciousness is rooted in, and feeds on, past times. The present moment is less important for it, it is only a gateway leading to a future we long for. Future is nothing but an improved and beautified version of the past, a future in which we will be successful in all of the things in which we have failed in the past. For ordinary consciousness, only past and future exist, it lives in those and feeds on those.

In that state of Consciousness the appreciation and opinion of others are very important for us. We want to meet the expectation directed at us, and we are pleased to play the social roles that are dictated by our community. We thrive to be good parents, a good husband or wife, useful employees and law abiding citizens. Our willingness to play these roles is caused by our complete identification with those roles. Our entire identity is based upon those roles. We do not look for true answers to the question" Who am I?;" we are content to be told that by others.

In the state of ordinary Consciousness, the dominant character of our life is the Ego; we wish to make it larger, brighter and more individual. That is why we are learning, gathering knowledge from others, until the end of our life, in the belief that we will thus become more and more intelligent. Still, we become less and less self-confident, and we do not have enough courage to face the challenges of life on our own. We therefore need a guide, a support. We do not long for complete freedom, we follow pre-determined rules and respect authority.

The Level of Awakening

The advent of that level is indicated by moments in our life when we wake up from our ordinary life, and recognize the reality that we in fact live in the captivity of our thoughts, emotions and social roles. Under the effect of those moments, a profound desire for freedom and truth arises in us. We then begin to search for the paths leading to the desired freedom. We intend to become more conscious and alert, to find the truth for ourselves about who we are and what our mission in the world is.

We no longer want to obey the old rules, old leaders, traditions and authorities. We no longer accept ready-made, second-hand theories and explanations. We are not ready to depend on the opinion of others any more. Instead, we want to acquire knowledge and experience from the world for ourselves. We take pleasure in discovering new things, and we embark on new journeys without fear.

It is at that level that real self-control is created in us. This self-control is not rooted in fear of punishment or hope of reward. Many people are able to develop a high degree of self-control in the fear of Hell or the hope of Heaven, or merely because they want to work together with something they regard as larger than themselves. That kind self-control will, however, only produce temporary results, since it is based upon suppression. Its maintenance requires constant effort from us. If, for some reason, the degree of effort declines, the suppressed desires, anger and emotions burst out, causing us even more suffering.

Real self-control is not born in us out of suppression, but out of the recognition and understanding of the meaning of Life. That kind of self-control will liberate our Consciousness from the state of identification with the world of Shapes and Forms. It will create a space between us and the functions of the Mind, and in that space the ability of seeing and understanding will be born.

Real self-control does not have any rules, and there is nobody around to tell us how to do that. Everybody must create that self-control in themselves without any external pressure, putting aside all kinds of authorities, and using their own personal experience. Everything created for us by others is transitory, but what we create for ourselves will be lasting and permanent. Everybody must find himself or herself what he or she is looking for.

The Level of Complete Freedom

This is the highest peak in the evolution of the Consciousness. The most important characteristic feature of this level is alertness, the acceptance of the present moment, an openness to the existence, and a celebration of life.

In that state of Consciousness an entirely new dimension of existence opens up for us, showing us Existence from a completely new perspective. The unity behind the controversies is revealed in front of our eyes, and we no longer insist on looking on the sunny side of life, as we are able to discover beauty on the dark side, too.

We accept life as it is, and it is not done under pressure, since that acceptance is the result of our complete freedom. The freedom is, in turn, a fruit of our escape from the world of Shapes and Forms. We have understood and experienced the process of awakening. The time has come for us to take control over our mind whenever it is required by the circumstances. When we do not need the work of the mind directly, let us give it some rest.

Everything will be quiet and peaceful in us. We are beyond all good and evil, we are a mere Consciousness that does not analyze or judge, only contemplates. We realize that the same contemplating soul lives in everybody, so the differences between human beings are only superficial, and deep inside we are all the same. Experiencing that unity will bring us the ecstasy of Life, the perfect joy of Existence.

The Enlightenment

The ultimate goal of our spiritual quest is enlightenment, that is what we all wish to achieve. But why do we seek enlightenment? Perhaps because at present we feel that we are not yet what we should rightfully be, we are not yet enlightened. What can be the reason why we are under that impression? In the first years of our life it never occurred to us that we needed to change, we needed to become somebody else, that we were in need of enlightenment. Then, some time during our life, that urge arose in us. It is imperative that we examine the circumstances and reasons why that emotion appeared in us, since it is that very emotion that prevents us from becoming enlightened.

Enlightenment is not a remote state of Consciousness that we need to achieve some time in the future, but it is the very heart of our nature. Our spiritual quest, however, diverts our attention to that imaginary, future state of Consciousness that we believe to be enlightenment. In this way, the spiritual quest detaches and diverts us from our true nature, enlightenment. We are therefore unable to ever reach enlightenment through the process of spiritual quest.

Enlightenment is, as we can now see, our true, inner nature. But what is in our true, inner nature? Unfortunately, during our spiritual search, most of us have been alienated from it; so much so, that we have even forgotten about it. It is, however, permanently present in our life, but we simply disregard it. Our attention is always engaged by something, something that we need to deal with, so we very rarely take the trouble of looking into ourself. Still, if we were able to concentrate our attention on ourselves, that brief moment of alert Consciousness would be enough for us to recognize that the alert Consciousness, free of emotions and thoughts is our true inner nature. We are now enlightened, we have never been anything else.

The question now arises, where did that enlightenment, that alert consciousness disappeared to from our life? As children, playing free of problems, we live in the present moment, in the state of alert Consciousness (so if we wish to meet an enlightened human being, all we need to do is go out to the nearest playground).

Then, carefree playing was replaced by more serious things in our life. From our parents we learned who we are and what our mission in life is. We were told that we are young human beings, still in the process of developing and shaping, and becoming an adult is a hard work.

Carefree playing was gradually replaced by purpose-oriented work in our life. Our teachers and parents therefore taught as how to set up objectives, how to make plans, and we soon learned that future is more important for us than the present. We then concentrated our attention from the vividness of the present moment onto the image our parents and teachers created in us, onto the image we need to become one day. Simultaneously with that process, the impression that we are not what we are supposed to be emerged gradually in our mind.

As children we simply had no choice, we had to accept the process, we had to identify with the new image. We are therefore moving away from our own inner nature, under the hypnotic attraction of a future goal to be achieved later. It is thus understandable that we look upon enlightenment as a goal to be achieved in the future.

Spurred by our ambitions, we pursue various goals all through our lives. Our whole life is a rush. We chase our desires and unfulfilled dreams. We are attracted by money, power, prestige, a wholesome, happy life. We aspire for something all the time, we always want to achieve something. This restless rush is instigated by our fear that we are still not what we want to be. We are never satisfied, we always want something else, we would like to be better, more beautiful, richer than we are at present.

Everybody nurtures an idealized image of what he/she would like to be like. The mind projects this idealized image into the future, and reveals the way leading to it. But this image requires a constant rush, stress, anxiety and worry in our life, as nothing is free, we have to struggle to achieve our goals.

But this is not our own personal tragedy, but that of the entire mankind. Generation after generation is conditioned to that attitude by the preceding generations. It is a vicious circle, and breaking out of it is almost impossible.

During our spiritual journey we must recognize this process, and we must realize that we no longer need to become something new, as we are all in possession of all the qualities that we have been pursuing so far in our dreams.

We must make efforts to be present at every moment of our life. That Presence shall bring alert Consciousness back to our life. In the state of alert Consciousness thoughts will no longer keep our attention in captivity, and we may experience silence. In the alert silence we recognize that it is our real Self is, it is our real inner nature. Enlightenment is us, we ourselves.

Submerged into the Quiet of Consciousness

Let us take a closer look at that, how are the deeper dimensions of Alertness increase their presence in you, and how are you able to get from the state of consciousness meaning" I am this and that" to the state" I am," how can you replace active meditation with real meditation?

Let us start by observing that in every waking moment you experience that you exist, you are. This experience is, however, so common and familiar that you do not dwell on it too long. Instead, you are preoccupied by "who are you" and "what are you."

That is how your entire life story is born:" What was I, what will I be, what I want to become". The Ego-dominated mind keeps revolving around these questions, creating the psychological categories of time, the past and the future.

The fact that you exist means that you are alert. The fact that you are conscious and alert is the result of the pure Consciousness in you! In the following we wish to experience that pure Consciousness, we want to enable that Consciousness to awaken to its own existence in and through us.

Once you are able to keep your attention on the object of your meditation, now try to divert your attention from it to the space in which the object of your attention appears.

Then a new dimension of Alertness opens up in you. The space thus opening and the Presence appearing in it are now there for you to observe, your attention is able to grab them. You experience that you are Consciousness, sensing the work of the mind.

Now shift your attention to that contemplating Consciousness, to the "I exist," to the pure Presence. Try to find the core of the Consciousness, the idea of" I am," and who the person who has done the meditations before really is.

Submerge completely in the feeling of" I am," allow it to remain in itself, prevent it from being connected to thoughts and ideas, to the works of mind. Try to find the silence, the quiet of" I am," and stay within that.

In the meanwhile, try to locate Consciousness itself. Do not only watch what you are looking at, but also from where and with what intensity are you looking at it? In what quality are you watching? Who are you in the process of observation?

Be in the state from which recognition emerges, be at the source of recognition, where you are able to see recognition itself. Be in Sight itself.

Do not worry about the operations of your mind, just stay in the sensation of" I am." Do not qualify, do not interpret! Stay in the sensation of" I am."

Whenever your attention wanders away, trying to get into contact with thoughts, trying to be manifested in some story, bring it back to the state of" I am," and keep it there.

"Through the Gate of the ALERTNESS
Leave Behind Yourself, the EGO
And Return to Your Spiritual Home
to the shining CONSCIOUSNESS"
(Wanderer's Sutra)

About the Author

Frank M. Wanderer
(Ph.D, Prof. of Psychology, consciousness researcher, writer)

The awakening of the Consciousness leads us from our own personal history to the pure space of Consciousness. There we experience the Miracle, and all personal histories become insignificant. Despite this, I would like to present a few pages of my personal history to the reader, as every journey on the road starts with a personal history. That is the only way it may start, there is no alternative; that is the only way leading to the awakening of the Consciousness, the appearance of the Miracle.

Since my early childhood, I have been interested in the Miracle, the mystery of human existence, the *mystery that summoned us from the Nothing, and the mystery we are destined to solve in our life*.

I still remember my beloved mother's astonished face when, after some of my questions, she turned to the others: "Now, look at that, what that kid is asking!"

The questions did not stop in the later years but, as I did not find an appropriate partner from whom I could expect answers, the questions mostly remained within the walls of my room, and I myself attempted to find the answers.

My motivation became even more powerful after the following adventure: I was at the elementary school (12 years old), walking home from school and suddenly I experienced the Miracle, the completeness, the experience of the unity with the Self. At that time, naturally, I was not able to describe it that way, but the sense of unity and happiness was what I experienced.

That experience did not result in my lasting awakening, it faded away after a while, but it left behind a burning wound, a real sense of want. At the same time, it showed me the way where to look for the answers to my questions. There was a long way to go until the second awakening. The first awakening made me start dealing with esoterica and find books on the subject.

Leaving the years of childhood behind, in my adulthood I became intensively interested in the human soul, in the work of the human mind.

As a teacher and psychologist I have met a lot of people, and had an opportunity to study the" normal" operation of the human ego, and also its functions that are considered as not normal. I turned the pages of innumerable books of personal histories, trying to find the cornerstones that give the dramas and ecstasies of these personal histories meaning and sense.

I eventually found that cornerstone in the Miracle, in the awakening of the Consciousness, which demonstrated the futility of these personal histories and at the same time it showed the treasure to be found in them.

The personal histories are futile from the aspect of the awakening because we identify with our mind and we allow its unconscious functions to control our life and steer the boat of our life in one, and some time later just the opposite direction, depending on the actual desire or ambition dominating our mind. That is how page after page is filled in the history of our life until the last page arrives, and we realize the futility of all that happened before.

Our personal history may, however, have a very profound meaning if we become more wakeful and alert to these mind games, and recognize the Miracle, the wide open spaces of the Consciousness that is beyond our personal history. That pure consciousness was what I experienced as a child, and that is what I found again as a result of my regular meditation exercises that I had started a few years ago.

We must therefore wake up from our identification with our personal history, so as to be able to find our identity in the Miracle, the mystery of the Consciousness, instead of the world of the forms and shapes.

Homepage:
http://powerofconsciousness.blogspot.com

https://fmwanderer.wordpress.com/

Email: margif61@gmail.com

Please consult our books on Consciousness at
http://amazonbooks.kery.org

PUBLISHED BOOKS ON
AMAZON.COM

Frank M. Wanderer

The Awakening
of Consciousness

Adventures On The Spiritual Path

FRANK M. WANDERER: THE AWAKENING OF CONSCIOUSNESS

Paperback: 122 pages
Publisher: CreateSpace Independent
Publishing Platform (January 14, 2014)
Language: English
ISBN-10: 1495200558
ISBN-13: 978-1495200557
Product Dimensions: 6 x 0.3 x 9 inches

We are all on a spiritual journey. This journey starts with birth and ends with death. Our life is a link between our date of birth and date of death. A link that contains all the secrets, dramas, tragedies and comedies of our lives, and we are so deeply involved in this performance that we tend to forget who we really are: the shining Consciousness. This book is about this spiritual journey.

Search on amazon for it or visit
http://fmw.kery.org

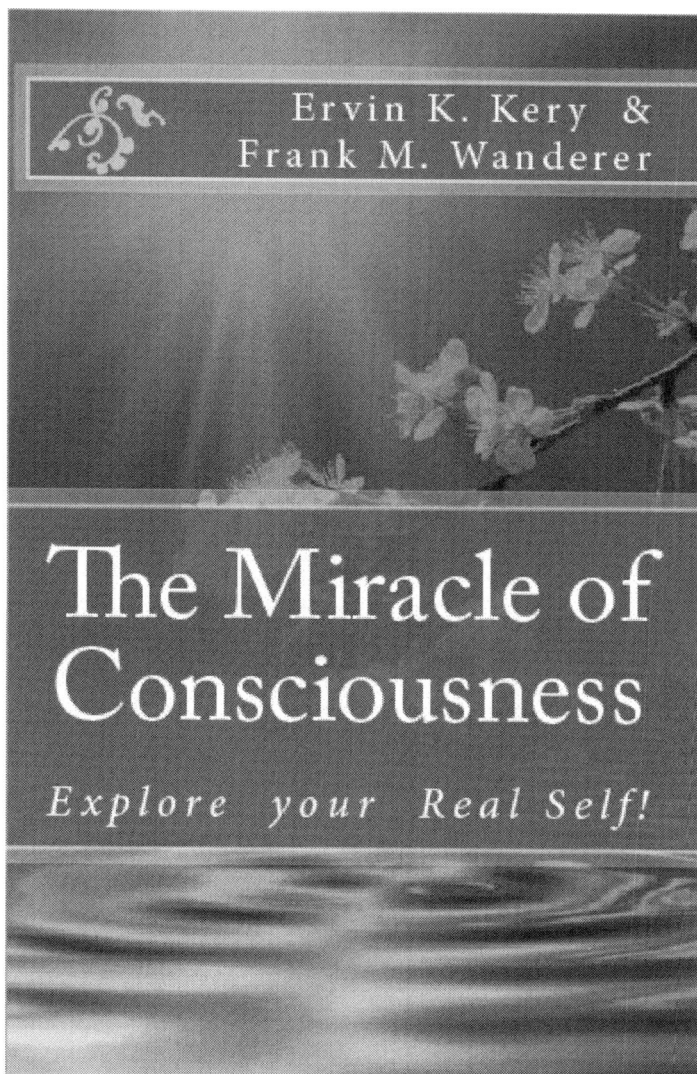

Ervin K. Kery &
Frank M. Wanderer

The Miracle of Consciousness

Explore your Real Self!

ERVIN K. KERY & FRANK M. WANDERER:

THE MIRACLE OF CONSCIOUSNESS

Paperback: 158 pages
Publisher: CreateSpace Independent
Publishing Platform; 1 edition (June 4, 2014)
Language: English
ISBN-10: 1499115458
ISBN-13: 978-1499115451
Product Dimensions: 5 x 0.4 x 8 inches

There is a mysterious human dimension, the recognition of which shatters all our ideas about who we are, where we come from and what our mission in this world is. This is the realm of Consciousness: the final scientific and spiritual mystery. This book is about the mysteries and miracles of Consciousness. About the living spirit in action which, dressed up in the machinery of your body, discovers itself and the wonders of the world.

Search on amazon for it or visit
http://fmw.kery.org

Frank M. Wanderer

The Flames of Alertness

Discover the Power of Consciousness!

FRANK M. WANDERER: THE FLAMES OF ALERTNESS

Paperback: 68 pages
Publisher: CreateSpace Independent Publishing Platform; 1 edition (October 8, 2014)
Language: English
ISBN-10: 1502748339
ISBN-13: 978-1502748331
Product Dimensions: 5 x 0.2 x 8 inches

This book will only reach you if a tiny flame of Alertness is burning in you. This awakening, small flame will be fanned up into a huge, blazing torch in you, and that torch will devour the accustomed, isolated world around you and place you back into the Oneness, which is your natural state of existence.

Search on amazon for it or visit http://fmw.kery.org

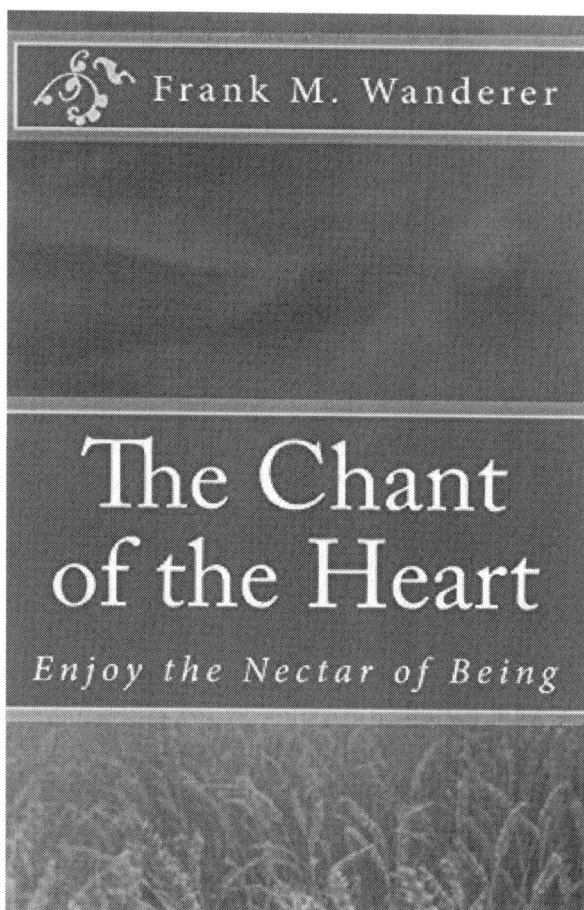

FRANK M. WANDERER:

The Chant of the Heart (Enjoy the Nectar of Being)

Paperback: 136 pages

•**Publisher:** CreateSpace Independent Publishing Platform (September 18, 2015)
•**Language:** English
•**ISBN-10:** 1517393124
•**ISBN-13:** 978-1517393120
•**Product Dimensions:** 5 x 0.3 x 8 inches

When our alertness is intensified, we begin to realize that we are not a body and a soul, but a pure, contemplating Consciousness behind these. A great inner awakening takes place in us and, for the first time in our life, we begin to feel the most elementary truth of our life, and we experience the pure joy of Existence. The chant of the heart will sound in us, and our love and happiness will overflow, pouring out to the outside world. The chant will be a wake up call for the people around us, helping them to find their own harmony in themselves, so that they may also sing the chant of the heart.

Look for it at http://fmw.kery.org

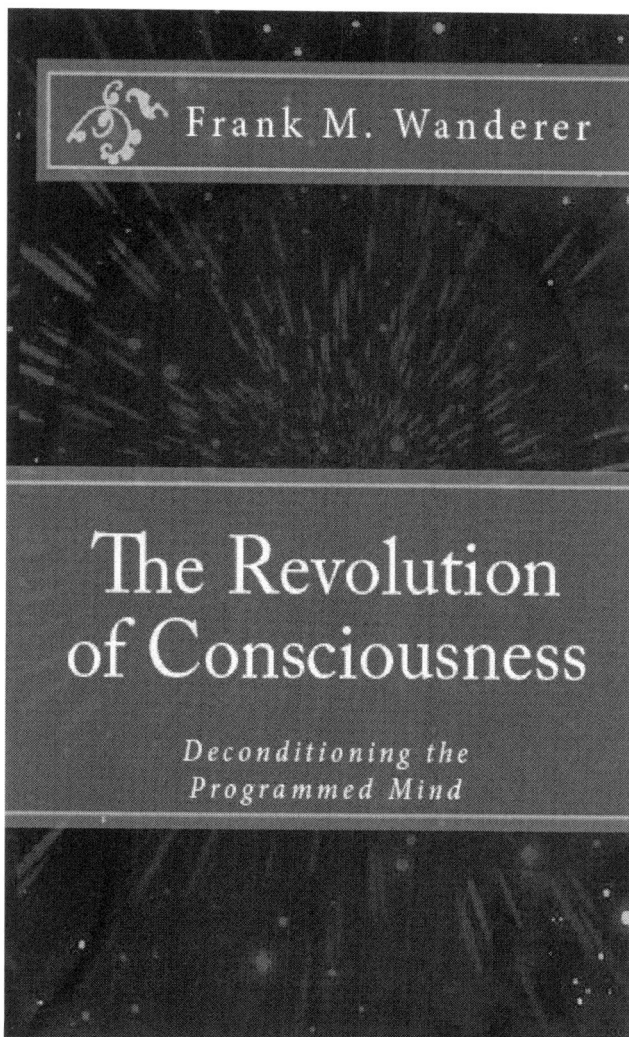

FRANK M. WANDERER:

The Revolution of Consciousness:
(Deconditioning the Programmed Mind)

Paperback: 96 pages

•**Publisher:** CreateSpace Independent
Publishing Platform; 1 edition (May 24, 2015)
•**Language:** English
•**ISBN-10:** 1512333913
•**ISBN-13:** 978-1512333916
•**Product Dimensions:** 5 x 0.2 x 8 inches

The revolution of the Consciousness is taking
place Now, in the present moment. There are
no strategies, no great leaders in this
revolution, only heroes who understand the
evolutionary progress of the Consciousness
and are open to allow the processes to take
place in themselves

Search on amazon for it or visit
http://fmw.kery.org

*FOR MORE BOOKS AND EBOOKS
AUTHORED BY FRANK M. WANDERER*

PLEASE VISIT http://FMW.KERY.ORG

19167905R00080

Printed in Great Britain
by Amazon